Using
Shared Reading Fiction
to Teach Essential Skills

Table of Contents

What Is Shared Reading? 3

How Shared Reading Works 6

Organizing Your Classroom 9

Selecting Texts. 11

Conducting a Shared Reading Lesson. 14

Phonological Awareness Mini-Lessons 21

Phonics Mini-Lessons 25

Vocabulary Mini-Lessons 29

Comprehension Mini-Lessons. 32

Fluency Mini-Lessons 44

Bibliography 47

. . . your students will likely clamor for you to "Read it again!" as they come to consider the story a familiar and trusted friend.

What Is Shared Reading?

Shared reading is a collaborative experience that allows all students in a classroom to engage in the reading process, regardless of their reading levels or reading abilities. As the teacher and students read together, challenging texts become accessible, and students build experience with the written word and strengthen their problem-solving abilities. While all of this is occurring, the teacher cheerfully models the practices and thought processes of a good reader, and provides in-depth strategy instruction as well.

Shared reading typically uses oversized Big Books with enlarged print and illustrations that every student can see and enjoy even when sitting toward the back of the room. Shared reading books are specifically designed to consider the needs of children at the emergent and early stages of reading development. The stories feature rhythm, rhyme, and rich language that students will want to read again and again. Shared reading can also include poetry, songs, and even expository texts. Vivid illustrations and large, appealing photographs keep the students' attention.

During a shared reading, you (the teacher) read the text out loud, pointing a finger or sweeping a hand under the words, inviting the students to follow along. Some children may participate only at the listening level, while others read along with you. Reading in unison gives the students confidence: They are supported by their peers rather than being isolated and worried about making a mistake. Along the way, you stop to think aloud about the strategies that help a reader better understand the text, artfully crafting the lesson to provide the necessary structure for a successful experience. You then reread the text over a period of days or even weeks to model additional reading and thinking strategies, always with a specific focus in mind. But don't worry—no one will tire of the book. In fact, your students will likely clamor for you to "Read it again!" as they come to consider the story a familiar and trusted friend.

Even students in the earliest phases of a reading program can take pleasure in rich, authentic, compelling literature that their word-identification skills would not otherwise allow them to access. In addition:

- Students are able to see firsthand what quality writing looks and sounds like.

- Students develop basic reading concepts and learn how print works.

- Students learn to recognize letters, words, and language patterns as they interact with the text.

- Teachers have multiple opportunities to model fluent reading and problem-solving strategies.

Read-Aloud vs. Shared Reading

Shared reading replicates many of the benefits of the familiar bedtime reading experience children enjoy at home. However, shared reading is different from a typical read-aloud session.

In a Read-Aloud	In Shared Reading
You read the text.	You and the students read the text.
You have the only copy of the text.	You use a Big Book, individual books, handouts, a chart, an overhead, or a whiteboard display so everyone in the class can see and interact with the text.
You have the sole responsibility for modeling thinking through the text.	Students share the responsibility for thinking aloud based on your prompts.
You read the text through one time.	You read the text over and over again.

Frequently Asked Questions

Why is shared reading so important?

Shared reading gives students the opportunity to work with a text in a nonthreatening way while developing a strong foundation for small-group and independent reading. The voluntary nature of shared reading invites students to take greater risks while scaffolded by their peers and the teacher's thinking and modeling. Shared reading also supports learners through different modalities, such as Big Books, small books, audio CDs, and whiteboard displays.

How much time should I devote to shared reading?

Shared reading should be a daily component of your comprehensive literacy program. However, the time devoted will vary from day to day depending on the text and the depth of your strategy instruction. Most shared reading blocks range from 20–25 minutes.

How can I use shared reading in the content areas?

By using nonfiction texts for your shared reading experiences, you can easily integrate content into your reading instruction. Students need good models for strategy instruction in different genres of text, and shared reading provides an excellent opportunity to think aloud and model the strategies you want them to learn.

How Shared Reading Works

Shared reading provides the opportunity for you to involve your students in the text and focus on a variety of aspects, both visual and cognitive. Both you and your students have important roles.

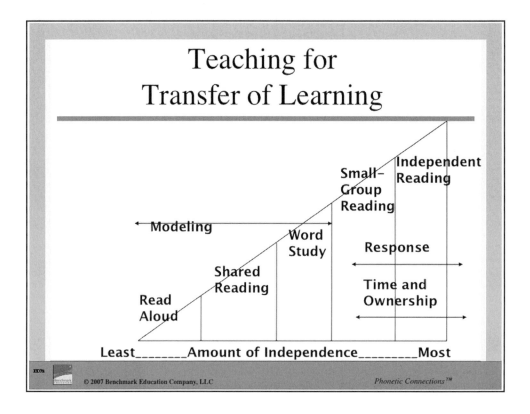

Teaching for Transfer of Learning

© 2007 Benchmark Education Company, LLC   *Phonetic Connections*™

As a result of shared reading, students will improve their abilities to choose appropriate, interesting texts for independent reading, and develop literacy skills in the essential areas of phonological awareness, phonics, vocabulary, comprehension, and fluency. Refer to the Responsive Teaching Prompts chart on page 8 for four levels of prompts you can use to support students from initial learning through successful implementation of a variety of strategies.

Gradual Release of Responsibility

We recognize that each student develops on an individual time line. When well planned and executed, shared reading is a developmentally appropriate way to differentiate instruction in a whole-group setting. As you gradually release responsibility, students begin to see themselves as co-readers. Drawn in by the text's content, students take on more and more active roles in the reading process.

Looking at the chart on page 6, you will notice that it is on a slant. When we reflect on our students as learners, we must think about the progression that all effective, active learning follows. You see something done, you have a chance to try it on your own with support, and then you are ready to try it by yourself. You followed the same model during your teacher preparation training. You didn't take over the whole class on the first day. First, you observed your cooperating teacher. Next, you tried a few things out while he or she was in the room to provide timely, on-the-spot feedback. Finally, you were responsible for all of the instruction with the whole class.

These are the same principles we apply to our students in learning to read. As students leave the comfort zone of shared reading, they are challenged in small-group settings, where they have even more responsibility for reading and applying what they have learned. While working in their instructional zone, they continue to receive strategy support from you on an as-needed basis.

The greatest amount of responsibility comes when students are reading independently. As a teacher, you have had the opportunity to hold their hands while showing them what to do, and now you expect them to stretch their wings and transfer their learning. All of the quality instruction you have provided is tested in the realm of independent reading.

Responsive Teaching Prompts

Whether teaching strategies for phonological awareness, phonics, vocabulary, comprehension, or fluency, teaching prompts must match your instructional focus and the students' needs.

Prompting Type	Purpose	Stems
Goal Oriented	Use these prompts for the reader who is not using the targeted strategy or skill at all. The prompts offer a model or a benchmark of how the strategy or skill is used in reading.	• Listen to how I . . . • Read it like this _____. • Watch how I . . . • _____ is not _____. • When I _____, I _____. • Notice what I do when I _____. • Describe/define _____. Point out example _____. • I'm going to _____. Listen to how I read this.
Corrective Feedback/ Directive	Use these prompts for students who are beginning to use the strategy or skill but still need direct teaching or coaching on how to use it properly.	• Now read _____. • Can you _____? • Do this _____. • Change this _____. • Try that again and _____. • Try doing this _____. • Repeat after me _____. • Read it like this _____.
Self-Monitoring/Reflective	Use these prompts for students who have previously exhibited use of the strategy or skill in reading but are not consistent. These prompts remind students to be more reflective and think about the importance of using the strategy or skill at the right time.	• How did you _____? • How did you know _____? • What did you notice about _____? • Did you have any trouble _____? • Was your reading _____ or _____? • I noticed _____. • When did you know to _____? • What made you _____? • Where did you _____?
Validating/Confirming	Use these prompts at any time to validate or confirm a student's reading strategies and skills.	• I like the way you _____. • Good job at _____. • You _____. • I noticed _____. • You took _____. • You made _____. • You are _____.

Organizing Your Classroom

Physical Space

Allot space for whole-group instruction in your classroom layout. Many primary classrooms use a carpeted area for a gathering spot. You will need a comfortable chair, a place to store instructional materials, and a place to display the texts to be read.

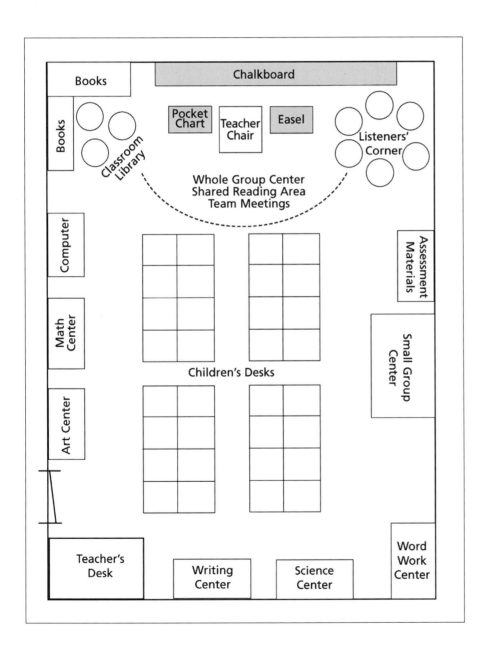

Materials

Since one goal of shared reading is to help students attend to the details of print, collect the following literacy tools in a handy basket:

- pointers

- highlighter tape

- sticky notes in a variety of sizes

- wax-covered yarn (such as Wikki Stix)

- framing cards and paddles

Use these instructional materials to highlight letters, letter clusters, known words, rhyming words, high-frequency words, punctuation, prefixes, suffixes, and other chunks of visual information. After focusing on one or two details, reread the text to put the visual pieces back into the context of a meaningful reading experience.

You will also want to have a chart or Big Book stand so your hands are free to point out things in the text. If needed, use clothespins to help hold pages open or attach the book to the stand.

Management

- Use a journal to keep track of the texts you use for shared reading. Document the title, author, and strategies modeled along with particular passages that were helpful to the lesson. Include any writing activities prompted by the lesson.

- Have students keep a class chart of the texts and strategies. This chart will enhance student responsibility and ownership for their learning.

- Keep a list of the strategy questions in a folder or on the wall in the area of the room where shared reading is most likely to occur.

- Display strategy charts and graphic organizers created during shared reading mini-lessons. Students can use these as resources during whole-group, small-group, and independent reading sessions.

- Keep a supply of new texts in the room as well as familiar favorites.

> *"The needs and interests of the children, the increase in complexity of language and language forms, the structure of the language, the layout and organization of text, the size and spacing of the print, and the topic all need to be considered in conjunction with the purposes the books will be used for. Above all, the books must delight the children and be worth returning to again and again."*
>
> **Brenda Parkes**, author of *Read It Again! Revisiting Shared Reading*

Selecting Texts

When thinking about what to teach during a shared reading lesson, carefully consider the various developmental levels of your students and their strengths and weaknesses. Reflecting on anecdotal records and your most recent assessment information will ensure that you are supporting reading development over time. You want to select texts that allow you to:

See the Annotated Features of Fiction Big Books for Primary Students on pages 12–13.

- demonstrate what fluent reading looks like and sounds like
- provide practice for strategies to make text understandable
- increase students' knowledge of language, themselves, and the world

A text used for shared reading should also have:

- rhyme, rhythm, and/or repetition
- literary qualities, such as strong characters or vivid descriptions
- an interesting story or topic that can hold students' attention over repeated readings
- easily remembered events that provide opportunities for art, writing, movement, drama, innovation, and language-based activities
- a mixture of supporting and challenging features

Before you select a text, ask yourself, *What teaching point(s) do I want to pull from the selection?* Then choose one of the following text options that show evidence of the skill or strategy:

- a Big Book
- a poetry chart
- an overhead transparency
- a whiteboard display
- a passage from a text (of which all the students have a copy)
- the lyrics to a song

Annotated Features of Fiction Big Books for Primary Students

- The large print type supports reading in a whole-group setting.

- The story lines are predictable and the text includes rhyme, rhythm, and/or repetition.

- Supportive illustrations help students recognize and understand the characters, setting, and plot.

" 'Tis only I, the littlest Billy Goat Gruff," called the first Billy Goat Gruff.

"I'M GOING TO COME AND EAT YOU UP!" roared the Troll.

6

• The spacing between words is exaggerated to encourage one-to-one matching.

"OH! Please don't eat me.
Wait for my brother,
the middle-sized
Billy Goat Gruff.
He's much bigger than
I am," replied
Little Billy Goat Gruff.

• Repetitive patterns utilize unusual placement, bold print, uppercase letters, and/or color to encourage participation and active engagement.

7

Conducting a Shared Reading Lesson

While there is no one correct way to implement shared reading, the typical lesson sequence is the introduction, a first reading, a second reading, and subsequent readings.

- The **introduction** builds background for reading the text.

- The **first reading** fosters students' enjoyment and comprehension of the text. Allow children to savor the words and illustrations without pressure to perform.

- The **second reading** encourages the students to participate more fully. You might want to focus on repetitive elements or chants and invite students to join you in the reading. Participation is voluntary and the emphasis should remain on meaning and enjoyment.

- The **subsequent readings** support students' reading development through explicit strategy instruction and promote a deeper understanding of the text. Once several stories have been introduced, ask students which are their favorites and pick those for rereading. At this stage, you should see increased participation, because this is now a very familiar text.

Introducing a Text

When introducing a text for the shared experience, your goal is to increase the students' desire to participate in the reading. Encourage them to share their thoughts about the text as well as their prior knowledge about the possible content. However, do not delay the first reading too long, or students will lose interest. Draw children into the book by using some of the following questions or prompts:

- What does the title make you think about? What can you picture in your mind?

- Look at the cover. I wonder why the author shows . . .

- What does the cover tell you about the characters in the story?

- Look at the title page. What do you see? Do you want to change any of your predictions?

- Where do you think this story takes place?

- What do you think will happen in the story?

Preplanning for a Shared Reading Lesson

There are several pre-lesson planning steps that, if followed closely, will make the shared reading experience beneficial to the teacher and students.

Choose a Purpose

The first step is to choose a purpose for the shared reading lesson. Teachers can choose to model a new strategy, revisit a previously modeled strategy, or review/reteach a previously modeled strategy to support readers who have not been able to transfer the strategy to independent work.

Choose a Strategy or an Essential Reading Element to Focus On

At the beginning of the year, use informal reading observation notes to determine students' strengths and weaknesses. Plan lessons based on those notes.

After spending some time getting to know students through individual conferences and small-group reading, identify their likes/dislikes and how well they are able to use strategies in a supportive environment. Plan lessons based on gathered information.

Read response journals to see how well students are able to use strategies independently. Plan lessons based on students' responses.

First Reading

The first reading should flow smoothly and without interruption except where students are confused and at risk of losing meaning. You can also briefly model predicting and confirming strategies as you turn the pages to maintain comprehension and interest. For example, say:

- I wonder what will happen to _____.
- I wonder if the next page will tell me _____.
- I think that _____ will happen next. I wonder if I am right.
- Let's read on and see if the author will tell us more about _____.

In addition, once you have established the rhythm or repeated structure of the text, you can invite students to join in, accepting all approximations and efforts.

Second Reading

Continue supporting students' comprehension while inviting them to participate in the text in whatever way they feel most comfortable. Occasionally pause to let students fill in an important word, phrase, or idea learned in the first reading. At the end, invite students to retell the story or information using art, writing, movement, drama, innovation, or language-based activities.

Subsequent Readings

You can utilize the third, and subsequent, shared reading to model and demonstrate a variety of strategies, including:

- directionality
- one-to-one matching
- locating known words and letters
- locating unknown words and letters based on letter/sound relationships
- rereading to monitor with meaning, structure, and visual cues
- predicting and confirming
- cross-checking one cue source against another
- searching for additional information
- self-correcting

Teacher Tip

At the end of the first reading, briefly comment or ask and answer questions to show how readers can reflect on a text. These remarks should not create a long discussion. Remember that you are modeling how readers think and not necessarily inviting a response.

Teacher Tip

See the charts on pages 18–20 for specific questions and prompts you can use to help students focus on targeted strategies.

Supporting Diverse Populations

English-Language Learners

Shared reading helps English-language learners make great gains by allowing students to see as well as hear the text and to practice reading in a nonthreatening atmosphere. Students should be encouraged—but not forced—to join in when they are able and to simply listen and attend to the text when they need more support. Multiple readings of the same text build even more confidence and willingness to participate. Remember that a student who has learned to read in his or her first language may have a much easier time making connections between oral and written words in the new language than a student who has not had this opportunity.

Special Needs Learners

Special needs learners can benefit from having a reading buddy during shared reading. Using paired reading, the special needs student reads aloud at the same time as his or her more accomplished buddy. When the special needs student feels ready, he or she signals the helper to stop reading and continues on alone. The helper then rejoins the reading at the student's next signal. Adult tutors, cross-age tutors, or peer tutors should be trained in advance to use the paired-reading approach.

Gifted and Talented Learners

After several teacher-led shared reading sessions, allow a gifted student or a small group of gifted students to present a shared reading lesson that you have helped them plan. This activity boosts self-esteem and public speaking. After the lesson is complete, check the students' understanding of the strategy that was modeled.

Target Reading Strategy Prompts

Teacher-directed prompts invite students to participate in reading. They also give teachers a way to assess students' progress. When revisiting texts to make or reinforce teaching points, prompts provide an opportunity to observe students interacting with the text. For example, the open-ended prompt "Show what you know" allows students to contribute without fear of being incorrect and gives you insight into the literacy knowledge they have under control (or believe they have under control). On the other hand, the more direct prompt "Who can show us _____?" allows students to contribute specific knowledge you request, helping you see who understands a concept and who might need further support. For this prompt, be prepared to accept approximations.

Use the charts below to select prompts in key reading-skills areas.

Concepts About Print	
Front of book	Where can we find the front of the book?
Difference between a picture and a page of print	Does this page have pictures or words on it?
One-to-one matching, left-to-right directionality, and return sweep	Who can help me follow along with a pointer?
Beginning and end	Where do we begin reading? Where do we finish?
Bottom of a picture	**Nonfiction:** What do we call these words below the picture? (caption) **Fiction:** Sometimes books will continue with words below pictures. We follow the text down the page even when it is below pictures.
Inverted page of print	Sometimes authors put the print in different places. Who can tell me what is different about this page of print?
Left page begins a text	Where do we begin reading? Sometimes an author puts words on the left page instead of beginning on the right side. It is important to always look for the title page and where the story begins.
Word order	Notice how the author used words in the sentence. Does the sentence start with a person, place, or thing? If it does, the author will then tell us what the person, place, or thing is doing.
Letter order	How would you start that word if you were writing it?

Making Connections

Text-to-self	How does the text remind you of your own experiences?
Text-to-text	How does the text connect to something else you have read?
Text-to-world	How does the text connect to the world around you?

Questioning

Constructing meaning	What do you think the story means?
Enhancing understanding	What other stories have you read that remind you of this one?
Finding answers	Where can we find the answer to _____?
Finding specific information	Let's go back and look for _____.
Clarifying confusion	This seems a little confusing. What facts from the story can we use to clarify what the author means?
Identifying research topics	We read about many things. What might we want to find out more about?

Visualizing

Creating mental images from text	Close your eyes. What do you see when you think about the story?
Placing yourself in text	If you were in the story, what would you do?
Stimulating imaginative thinking	Everyone close your eyes. Imagine you are _____ in the story. What would you do next?

Determining Text Importance

Remembering important information	This is very important. Let's mark this with a sticky note so we will remember it later.
Distinguishing what is important from what is interesting	What things are important in this story? What things are interesting?
Discerning a theme, opinion, or perspective	What is the moral of this story?
Determining if the author's perspective is to inform, persuade, or entertain	Why do you think the author wrote this story?

Making Inferences

Drawing conclusions	We finished reading _____. Can you come up with three words to describe _____? What in the story led you to use those three words?
Making predictions	What do you think will happen next in the story?
Using implicit information to make meaning	Page _____ says _____. What does that mean in this story?

Synthesizing Information

Stopping to collect your thoughts	Let's stop here and think about what we have read.
Summarizing information	How would you summarize this story?
Combining main points into big ideas	Let's combine all the main points into one big idea.
Making generalizations	Think about what we read. How would you describe _____?
Making judgments	What is your opinion of this book/story/passage?
Assimilating information	How would you put all this information together? What does it mean to you?

Teacher Tip

To further delve into students' thought processes, offer the following sentence starters for students to complete with a partner, in a small group, or in the whole-group setting:

I already know that . . .

We are reading this piece because . . .

When I think about this piece, I am reminded of . . .

When I hear this piece, I wonder about . . .

I am confused about . . .

I need to know more about _____ because . . .

I don't understand the word . . .

I don't understand why the character did . . .

I noticed this piece is organized like . . .

This picture is what I think the author meant when he wrote about . . .

The point of the piece is . . .

The author obviously thinks _____ is important because . . .

The author's words show me that . . .

I can help myself understand this book by . . .

Phonological Awareness Mini-Lessons

Phonological awareness is the ability to notice, think about, and work with the individual sounds in spoken words. Before children learn to read print, they need to become aware of how the sounds in words work. They must understand that words are made up of speech sounds, or phonemes. Phonological awareness fosters efficient reading.

The following shared reading activities provide explicit instruction at different levels of phonological awareness using pages 2–3 of the Big Book *Who's in the Shed?* by Brenda Parkes.

Down at the farm
one Saturday night,
the animals woke
with a **terrible** fright.

as something was led
from a truck
to the shed.

There was **howling**
and **growling**
and **roaring**
and **clawing**

"Who's in the shed?"
everyone said.
"Who's in the shed?"

Recite the Text

Help students learn a selected passage by reading or reciting it for them first. As you chant the words, emphasize the rhythm and the rhyming words. Next, reread the passage line by line and have students repeat each line back to you in unison. The initial pace will be slow. Pick up the speed as students gain mastery until a fast, fluent pace is attained. To maintain engagement, invite students to sing, clap, and act out the text as they recite it.

Word Awareness

Ask students to listen to one sentence from the passage. **Ask:** *How many words do you hear in this sentence?*

Sound Matching

1. Pronounce two words from the passage and ask students whether they begin the same. For example, **ask:** *Do **Saturday** and **something** begin the same way?*

2. Ask students to name two words in the passage that begin the same.

Sound Isolation

Using selected words from the passage, ask students to name the first sound of the word. For example, **say:** *Tell me the first sound in the word **terrible**. Tell me the last sound in the word **fright**.*

Phoneme Blending

Slowly articulate a word from the passage. Ask students to blend the word together. For example:

Teacher: /tr/ /u/ /k/

Students: truck

Sound Addition or Substitution

Choose a word from the passage. Ask students to add a new sound to make a new word. For example:

Teacher: Say the word **in**.

Students: in

Teacher: Put **/f/** in front of the word **in**. Tell me the new word.

Students: fin

Sound Segmentation

Choose selected words from the passage. Ask students to tell you what sounds they hear in each word. For example, say the word **and**. Then **ask:** *What sounds do you hear in the word **and**?*

Phoneme Manipulation

Ask students to manipulate phonemes from selected words in the passage. For example:

Teacher: Take away the first sound in **at**. Add **/i/**. What is the new word?

Students: it

Teacher: Take away the last sound in the word **led**. Add **/t/**. What is the new word?

Students: let

Word Rhyming

1. Stop after the rhyming words and ask students to say the words they heard in that rhyme.

2. Stop before reading the second word of a rhyming pair, and ask students to predict the word before you continue.

3. Name a word in the passage and ask students to tell you the word that rhymes with it. Follow up by asking how the two words are alike. For example:

> **Teacher:** Which word rhymes with **night**?
> **All: fright**
> **Teacher:** That's right. How are **night** and **fright** alike?
> **All: Night** and **fright** both end with the **/ite/** sound.

4. Divide the class into two groups. One group chants the passage but stops just before a rhyming word. The second group then shouts the rhyming word that completes the sentence. For example:

> **Group One:** Down at the farm one Saturday . . .
> **Group Two:** night!
> **Group One:** . . . the animals woke with a terrible . . .
> **Group Two:** fright!

5. To help students attend to discrepancies between what they expect to hear and what they do hear, ask them to close their eyes and give you a signal when they hear something wrong. Substitute a word, such as **car** for **truck** or **yelled** for **said**. Encourage students to explain what is wrong.

Clapping Syllables

1. Show students how to separate words into parts by clapping the syllables. Model by clapping the syllables in students' names. **Ask:** *How many syllables did you hear?* Then have students join you on words from the passage, such as:

> **One syllable:** down, farm, night, woke
> **Two syllables:** howling, growling, roaring, something
> **Three syllables:** Saturday, animals, terrible, everyone

2. Ask students which words are longer or shorter after they are clapped. Then compare their responses with the words in print.

Phonics Mini-Lessons

Phonics instruction teaches students the relationships between the letters (graphemes) of written language and the individual sounds (phonemes) of spoken language, and how to use these relationships to read and write words. Knowing these relationships will help students recognize familiar words accurately and automatically and decode new words.

Using shared reading, you can design mini-lessons that help beginning readers learn about letters, sounds, spelling patterns, and words. During these mini-lessons, use explicit language to prompt students to categorize, associate, link, and generalize information.

The following phonics mini-lessons are based on a shared reading of pages 12–13 of the Big Book *The Gingerbread Man* by Brenda Parkes and Judith Smith.

As he ran, he called,
 Run, run, as fast as you can.
 You can't catch me,
 I'm the Gingerbread Man.
The little old man and woman
 both ran after him.

The Gingerbread Man ran
past a boy and a girl.
"**Stop!**" cried the boy.
"**Stop!**" cried the girl.
But the Gingerbread Man ran **faster**
and **FASTER**.

12   13

Sounds and Letters

1. Help students compare and locate words that have the same sound and letter in the initial, medial, or final position. For example:

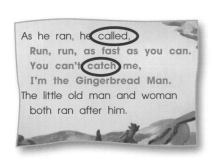

   Teacher: Let's look at page 12 in *The Gingerbread Man*. Let's reread the first four lines together.

   Students: As he ran, he called, "Run, run, as fast as you can. You can't catch me, I'm the Gingerbread Man."

   Teacher: *(The teacher points to the words **called** and **catch**.)* How are these two words the same?

   Students: They start the same.

   Teacher: Good checking! Yes, **called** and **catch** begin with the same sound. *(The teacher uses a framing card to highlight the **c** in **called** and **catch**.)* These two words start with the letter **c** just like one of the pictures on our alphabet chart. Who can find the picture?

   Tony: I can! **Cap!**

   Teacher: Yes! **Called** and **catch** do start like **cap** on the alphabet chart. *(The teacher hands a pointer to Tony.)* Go and point to that box on the alphabet chart while we read it.

   All: *(chanting)* **/C/, /c/, cap!**

   Teacher: **Called**, **catch**, and **cap** all begin the same. Who can find one more word on the page that starts like **called**, **catch**, and **cap**?

   Angela: I can! **Can!**

   Teacher: Super! **Can** begins with the same sound and letter as **called**, **catch**, and **cap**. *(The teacher hands Angela an appropriately sized framing card.)* Use this card to show me what letter in the word **can** makes the same beginning sound as **called**, **catch**, and **cap**. *(The student frames the **c** in **can**.)*

2. Activate students' knowledge of initial sounds and letters by having them locate words in the text that start with a specific letter. Write the words on a chart or on index cards to place in a pocket chart titled "Words That Start the Same." Add new words as you read new texts.

3. As students' knowledge of letters and sounds grows, extend the activity above by creating a list of words with the same middle sound and a list of words that end the same.

Onsets and Rimes

1. To extend students' ability to learn new words by analogy, help them manipulate patterns in their heads.

First, ask them to read the text fluently. Then ask them to name two words from the text that rhyme, such as **ran** and **man**. Next, prompt students to segment one of the words and identify it. For example, **ask:** *If I take /r/ from **ran**, what chunk is left?* (-an) Finally, ask students to put a new letter in front of the chunk to make a new word. For example, **say:** *Put /t/ in front of the chunk **-an**. What is the new word?* (tan)

2. Ask the students to locate a word in the text based on the information that you give. For example, **say:** *Find a word in the text that starts like **hat** and rhymes with **rim**.* The students would then locate the word **him**.

Spelling Patterns

1. Explain that a spelling pattern is the first vowel in a syllable and all the letters after it. Demonstrate by writing some familiar words on the board, such as **sit** and **bit**. Invite student volunteers to underline the spelling pattern (it).

2. To help students examine spelling patterns within a text, reconstruct part of the text in a pocket chart by writing each word on an individual index card. Have an empty pocket chart nearby. Here is a sample scenario:

Teacher: Let's look at the passage we just read. Who can find two words that rhyme?

Students: Can and **man**!

Teacher: Can and **man** do rhyme! Let's all say the words as Charlie gets the word cards out of the pocket chart.

Students: Can, man.

Teacher: Charlie, please put the words in the empty pocket chart. Can you tell us how the words are alike?

Charlie: The words sound alike, and both words have the **-an** chunk.

Teacher: That's right! You noticed that **can** and **man** both have the **-an** chunk. How could I use the words **can** and **man** to help me write the word **fan**?

Charlie: You could take off the **m** in **man** and put an **f** in front.

Teacher: Good job! I can keep the **-an** chunk from **man** and add an **f** to the beginning. *(The teacher quickly writes the word **fan** on the board.)* Now, let's see if **fan** looks like **can** and **man**. *(The teacher points to the word cards in the pocket chart.)*

Students: Yes!

Teacher: *(The teacher highlights the **-an** chunk in **fan** with a framing card.)* Yes, all the words have the **-an** chunk. Write **fan** on your practice board. *(The students write and check the word **fan**. The teacher writes **pan** on an index card and places it in the pocket chart with **can** and **man**.)*

Teacher: What if I were reading a story and I came to this new word? How could I figure it out?

Katie: It's **pan**!

Teacher: How do you know?

Katie: Because it has the **-an** chunk just like **can** and **man**. If you put **p** with the **-an** chunk, you get **pan**!

Teacher: That's super! We can use **can** and **man** to help us figure out **pan** because we know the **-an** chunk.

Teacher Tip

*Tell students that when they are reading or writing and come to a tricky word they don't know, they can think of other words they know that sound or look like the tricky word. In reading, **ask:** Do you know a word that looks like this word? In writing, **ask:** Do you know a word that sounds like this word?*

Vocabulary Mini-Lessons

Vocabulary refers to the words we must know to communicate effectively. Oral vocabulary is words we use in speaking or recognize in listening. Reading vocabulary is words we recognize or use in print. Vocabulary plays an important part in learning to read. As beginning readers, children use the words they have heard to make sense of the words they see in print. Vocabulary is also very important to reading comprehension. Readers cannot understand what they are reading without knowing what most of the words mean.

In *Bringing Words to Life: Robust Vocabulary Instruction*, Beck, McKeown, and Kucan categorize words into three tiers. The following mini-lessons demonstrate ways to teach each tier to emergent and early readers during a shared reading session using the Big Book *The Enormous Watermelon* by Brenda Parkes and Judith Smith.

One day Old Mother Hubbard went to the cupboard, but it was **bare**.

So she planted a little watermelon seed in the garden.

Each day Old Mother Hubbard looked at the watermelon. **"Grow, little watermelon,"** she said. **"Grow, big and sweet and juicy."** And the watermelon

grew

and **grew**

and **grew**

until it was

enormous.

Three Tiers of Vocabulary Instruction		
Tier	**Description**	**Example Words**
Tier One	Basic words	day, went, looked, said
Tier Two	Frequently used words in oral and written communications	bare, little, each, enormous
Tier Three	Infrequently used academic/content words referring to a particular subject or topic	planted, watermelon, seed, garden

Tier One

Write the words **day**, **went**, **looked**, **said** on an index card. Then:

1. Say one word aloud and run your finger under it as you say it.
2. Ask students to say the word with you.
3. Ask students to spell the word aloud as you point to each letter.
4. Invite students to write the word in the air as you point to each letter.
5. Discuss the meaning of the word in context.
6. Help students use the words in their own oral sentences.

Tier Two

Pronounce the word and ask students to repeat it. Provide a child-friendly definition of the word in the context of the text. Use the word in other contexts. Then invite students to share their ideas about the word. For example:

Teacher: Let's think about the word **enormous**. Say the word **enormous**.

Students: Enormous!

Teacher: The watermelon in the story is enormous. The watermelon is very, very large. Other things can be enormous, too. A skyscraper is enormous. A mountain is enormous. Some trees are enormous. What else can be enormous?

John: We have a little TV, but my uncle's TV is enormous!

Tamara: My mom and I went to an enormous store last Saturday!

Chris: My friend had a birthday party. The cake was enormous!

Teacher: Good thinking! What word have we been talking about?

Students: Enormous!

Teacher: Yes—**enormous**. Let's try to use the word **enormous** many times today. We can use the word at school and at home.

Tier Three

1. In *Building Academic Vocabulary*, Marzano and Pickering suggest a six-step approach to teaching Tier Three words:

1. Provide a description, explanation, or example of the new term.
2. Ask students to restate the description, explanation, or example in their own words.
3. Ask students to make a picture, symbol, or graphic of the term.
4. Engage students in activities that help them add to their knowledge of the term.
5. Ask students to discuss the term with one another.
6. Involve students in games that allow them to play with the term.

2. In the sample scenario, see how a teacher follows these steps to teach the word **garden** using the cover of *The Enormous Watermelon*.

Teacher: A garden is a place where people grow flowers, fruits, and vegetables. A garden can be in someone's yard. Imagine you are in a garden. What can you see? What can you hear? What can you smell? What can you feel? What can you taste?

Asa: I see dirt. I see daisies. I see green beans.

Nate: I am watering the plants. I hear the water hit the leaves.

Tess: I smell wet dirt. I smell a rose.

Sandy: I pick some tomatoes. They feel smooth.

Chloe: I pick some strawberries to eat. They are juicy.

Teacher: You have good imaginations! Now I will give each of you an index card. Draw part of a garden on your card. Then we'll tape the cards together and have a class garden. *(The teacher hands out the materials and allows time for the students to construct the garden.)*

Teacher: I have some books about gardens. Choose a book to look at with a partner. Then share one page of your book with the group. *(The teacher allows time for students to browse and share.)*

Teacher: Now we will play a game. I will name an object. You will give me a thumbs-up or thumbs-down to show whether you might see that object in a garden. *(The teacher names objects such as soil, a worm, a book, a flower, a dish, a pumpkin, a fence, a computer, and a leaf.)*

Teacher Tip

When you don't have time to go in-depth with a Tier Three word, utilize one of the following activities instead.

Concept Web—Write the word in the center of the board or chart paper, and ask students to brainstorm related words for you to record around it.

KWL Chart—Ask students to help you record what they know about the word and what they would like to learn. After studying the word, ask them to share what they learned.

Venn Diagram—Draw two overlapping circles and use them to compare two words.

Comprehension Mini-Lessons

Comprehension is the reason for reading. If readers can read the words but do not understand what they are reading, they are not really reading. Good readers have a purpose for reading: to think actively as they read. More than thirty years of research has shown that instruction in comprehension can help students understand, remember, and communicate with others about what they read.

Cloze Procedure

Use cloze procedure to assist students in applying prediction and cross-checking strategies. Prepare the text by using a sticky note to conceal words at various points. You and the students read the text up to the hidden word, and then the students are asked to make meaningful predictions. As students make their predictions, ask what letter(s) they expect to see at the beginning of their word. Record the word on the sticky note. Next, uncover the first letter(s) of the concealed word and assist students in confirming or rejecting their predictions based on the revealed letter(s). If needed, ask students to make new predictions. This technique assists you in helping students apply the following reading strategies: predicting, confirming, cross-checking, and searching.

One spring morning,
the little Red Hen
found a grain of wheat.
She asked the duck,
"Will you help me plant
this grain of wheat?"
"**Not I**," quacked the duck.
"I've got better things to do."

The following scenario is based on a reading of *The Little Red Hen* by Brenda Parkes and Judith Smith and illustrates the use of cloze procedure.

Teacher and Students: *(reading together)* "One spring _____, the Little Red Hen found a grain of wheat."

Teacher: When do you think Little Red Hen found the grain of wheat?

Beth: One spring day!

Harrison: One spring morning!

Teacher: *(validating)* Day and morning are good guesses. Day and morning both make sense. What letter would you expect to find at the beginning of the word **day**?

Students: D.

Teacher: What letter would you expect to find at the beginning of the word **morning**?

Students: M. *(The teacher writes the students' predictions on the sticky note.)*

Teacher: Let's check on ourselves by looking at the first letter of the word. *(The teacher reveals the first letter of the concealed word. She then points to the word **day** on the sticky note.)*

Teacher: *(pointing back to the story)* Could this word be **day**?

Students: No!

Teacher: Why?

Students: Because it doesn't have a **d** at the beginning. *(The teacher draws a line through the word **day** and points to the word **morning**.)*

Teacher: Could this word be **morning**?

Students: Yes!

Teacher: Why?

Students: Because it starts with the letter **m**.

Teacher: What other letters would you expect to find in the word **morning**?

Some Students: O and **r** like the word **or**.

Some Students: An **n**.

Some Students: The **ing** chunk.

Teacher: *(uncovering the hidden word)* Does this word look like **morning**?

Students: Yes!

Teacher: *(activating)* Does **morning** make sense in the text?

Students: Yes!

Teacher: Good thinking! You found two ways to help yourself. When you come to a tricky part, ask yourself, *Does it look right? Does it make sense?*

Metacognitive Strategies

Metacognitive strategies are specific thinking strategies used by proficient readers. Research has shown that reading is an interactive process whereby the reader engages in a constant internal dialogue with the text. This ongoing dialogue helps the reader understand and elaborate on what is being read. Shared reading provides many opportunities for teachers to direct students' attention to build on past knowledge, explore new information, and connect with the author's mind and intended message through think-alouds and focused prompts. Explicit teaching of these metacognitive strategies will give students access to information across the curriculum.

1. **Visualize** Proficient readers create many sensory images as they read. These mental images help the reader connect with the text emotionally. They help the reader to "get inside the author's head" to fully understand the message. Here is a modeled example of how to get students to visualize during a shared reading of *The Three Billy Goats Gruff* by Brenda Parkes and Judith Smith.

The great big Billy Goat
stopped still.
DOWN went his horns,
and he rushed at the Troll.
He butted him *once*
twice
three times.

The Troll tumbled off
the bridge,

down

down

down

into the deep water
under the bridge.

20

21

Teacher: When good readers read, they visualize, or see, pictures of the story in their mind. This helps them connect with the story and understand it at a deeper level. For example, I can just see the mean troll watching for the big billy goat to cross the bridge. He is ready and waiting for him. That troll thinks he can scare anyone. I can also see the ferocious look on his face. I can hear his voice, too. It is loud and harsh.

Now, the big billy goat is crossing the bridge. He isn't scared of anyone. I can see him walking boldly across the bridge. When the troll comes up, the big billy goat doesn't even flinch. I can just see him stopping still and butting the troll with his big horns. I can also hear the troll screaming for help as he falls far, far below.

Now I can see the big billy goat strolling gently over the bridge to be with his brothers. He is very calm.

> ### Teacher Tip
>
> **Prompts for Visualizing/ Creating Images**
>
> *The author gives me a picture in my mind when he describes . . .*
>
> *I can really see what the author is talking about when he . . .*
>
> *I can draw a picture of what the author is describing.*

2. Ask Questions Good readers generate questions before, during, and after reading to clarify and to focus on obtaining the author's message. Again, shared reading is the perfect opportunity to show the process of modeling what good readers do.

When reading with students, model how good readers ask questions as they read. For example, after reading the line "DOWN went his horns, and he rushed at the Troll," **say:** *I wonder what the word* **rushed** *means. I know that when you are in a hurry, you rush. I know the big billy goat was fighting off the troll. I am going to read the next sentence to see if I can find out more information.* Read the line "He butted him once, **twice**, **three** times," then **say:** *Now I think the word* **rushed** *means that the big billy goat went toward the troll boldly. I think that the word* **rushed** *means to go after something. Asking questions as I read helps me to understand the story better.*

> ### Teacher Tip
>
> **Prompts for Asking Questions**
>
> *I wonder why . . .*
>
> *What does this word mean?*
>
> *Why did _____ do that?*
>
> *What questions do I have before, during, and after reading?*
>
> *What is going to happen next?*
>
> *Why did the author put that part in there?*

Prompts for Making Inferences

The author says this, but means . . .

If I read between the lines, the author is telling me that . . .

The clues to prove my inference are . . .

Because of what the author said, I know that . . .

From the clues or information the author gives, I can conclude that . . .

I think that _____ will happen next because the author says _____.

3. Make Inferences Good readers use their knowledge of what they read to make predictions, draw conclusions, and create interpretations of the text to have a deeper understanding of the text. Here is a modeled example of making inferences using *Who's in the Shed?* by Brenda Parkes.

Read pages 10–11, and then prompt students to study the hen's expressions, first on page 10 before she looks in the shed and then again on page 11 after she looks in the shed. **Say:** *If I look at the hen on page 10, she looks calm as she is about to look in the shed. Now, on page 11, she looks frightened or surprised. From the look on her face I think there is some kind of scary creature in the shed.* Explain that clues from the picture are helping you think about what could be in the shed.

4. Making Connections Good readers use their background knowledge before, during and after reading to deepen their understanding of the story or text. Connections can be made text-to-self, text-to-text, or text-to-world.

After reading *The Enormous Watermelon* with students, ask students to make connections to the characters in the story, allowing responses between questions.

Teacher: Who were the characters in this story? Have you heard of these characters before? Where have you heard of them? Did reading about Little Miss Muffet make you think about the nursery rhyme about her? What other connections did you make with the story? Have any of you ever planted a garden? When good readers read, they make connections with something that has happened to them in the past, with another book they have read, or even something that is happening in the real world. Making connections helps us understand the author's message.

Old Mother Hubbard cut up the watermelon.

Then Old Mother Hubbard and Humpty Dumpty and Little Miss Muffet and Jack and Jill and Wee Willy Winky all sat down to eat it.

24

Teacher Tip

Prompts for Making Connections

This reminds me of a time when I . . .

I know about this topic because I . . .

The setting of the book is just like . . .

This book is something like . . .

What's going on in this book is just like what's happening in the _____.

Teacher Tip

Prompts for Synthesizing

This story or passage is really about . . .

I first thought _____ about the story. Now I think . . .

5. Synthesize Good readers pull all of the information together to enhance the overall meaning of the text or a story. To demonstrate the thought processes that go into synthesizing, here is a modeled example based on a reading of *Jack & the Beanstalk* by Brenda Parkes and Judith Smith.

Teacher: Wow, at first I thought that Jack and his mother were in big trouble because they had no cow and no money. I didn't see how Jack was going to get out of his trouble. Then I thought that he was in even more trouble with the Ogre. The story got pretty scary for a bit. However, now I think that Jack and his mother are safe. They also have the bag of gold, so they can buy food and they will not starve. They will have the things they need. At first, I thought Jack was very foolish, but now I see that he ended up being smart in outwitting the Ogre. After reading a story, good readers reflect on what they read. This helps them really think about all of the various things that went on in the story. It helps the reader understand what the author was saying.

Using Anchor Charts to Explicitly Teach Comprehension

During shared reading lessons, teachers introduce a strategy by offering a few ideas in writing, including defining the strategy and explaining how it helps readers. These notes are very valuable because they may be written on chart paper and hung on a wall for students to review when they are working in a small group, in pairs, or independently. This instructional strategy is a wonderful way to scaffold instruction while students learn how to use the modeled strategy independently. As students become independent, the chart (see the sample below) can be copied to regular-size paper and placed in the students' reading notebooks for continued use as needed. As lessons continue, add information to the chart that includes specific examples of text that help the readers visualize.

Strategy	Visualize
Definition	Using the words from the text to create a movie in your mind
About the Strategy	Visualizing helps me remember what I've read and makes the words more interesting, which makes me want to read more. I can create a movie from any genre including fiction, nonfiction, and poetry. Descriptive words and phrases help me visualize.

Sample Comprehension Anchor Chart

Graphic Organizers

Shared reading offers opportunities to teach emergent and early comprehension strategies through the use of graphic organizers and the gradual release method. First, think aloud and model the first few entries on the organizer. Next, guide students to help you select another entry or two. Finally, allow student-partners to come up with an entry to add. In this way, you gradually release responsibility and support students' growing toolbox of comprehension strategies. It is also important to explain why these comprehension strategies are important. For instance, they help us stay focused on what we are reading, make sense of what we are reading, and remember what we read.

Here are some simple graphic organizers you can create from *The Little Red Hen*.

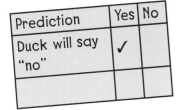

- **Make Predictions** Draw a three-column chart and label the columns **Prediction**, **Yes**, and **No**. Model how to make predictions before, during, and after reading. Then model how to use the text to confirm your predictions. If the prediction is confirmed, put a check mark in the **Yes** box. If you must revise your prediction, put a check mark in the **No** box. When using Big Books, many of the predictions will come from the pictures, and confirmations/revisions will come from both the pictures and the text. For instance, in *The Little Red Hen*, a reader might look at the picture of the duck and predict that he will say "No" because he does not look interested in what the hen has to say. In reading on, we find that the duck indeed does decline to help. Therefore, the prediction is confirmed.

- **Make Connections** Model how to connect the story to your own experiences (such as planting a seed—text-to-self), to what you already know (such as different types of animals that live on a farm—text-to-world), and to other books you have read (such as a fairy tale about animals—text-to-text). It's best to focus on only one type of connection at a time by creating a simple concept web or bulleted list.

- **Make Inferences** Draw a three-column chart and label the columns **Clues**, **What We Already Know**, and **Inference**. Model how to make an inference using one or two clues from the text combined with prior knowledge. In *The Little Red Hen*, the animals' refusal to help is a clue, and understanding that some jobs are easier to do with help is prior knowledge. We can put these together to infer that the animals are selfish or lazy.

- **Retell Facts** Draw a T-chart. In the first column, write simple questions about the text, such as *What did Little Red Hen find?* and *Why didn't the duck want to help?* Model how to use the key words in the question to locate the answers in the text, and record your answers in the second column.

- **Retell Story Elements** Create a story web. Label the center circle with the title of the text, and label the outer circles **Characters**, **Setting**, and **Plot**. Discuss the meaning of each story term and model how to find the information in the text. You can also use this opportunity to reinforce the strategy of making inferences. For example, in the Big Book we can use text clues and what we already know to infer that Little Red Hen lives on a farm.

- **Identify Sequence of Events or Steps in a Process** Using a series of boxes connected by arrows, model how to retell events or steps in time order. In the first part of the story, a hen finds a grain of wheat; the duck will not help; the dog will not help; the cat will not help; and the pig will not help. So the hen plants the grain of wheat herself. Once students know the entire story, you can extend learning by asking students to help you identify the steps in making bread from planting a seed through eating the finished product.

- **Identify Cause and Effect** Draw a simple two-column chart. In each row, write a cause in the first column and an effect in the second column. Model the process carefully, explaining that a cause comes first and an effect happens as a result of the cause. Examples of cause-and-effect relationships in *The Little Red Hen* include:

Cause: The hen finds a grain of wheat.	**Effect:** She decides to plant it.
Cause: The animals say they will not help.	**Effect:** The hen plants the grain of wheat herself.

- **Compare and Contrast** Draw a three-column chart or a Venn diagram. Label the first column or circle with the first thing to be compared, the middle column or intersecting area of the circles with **Both**, and the last column or circle with the second thing to be compared. In *The Little Red Hen*, students could compare the hen and the duck. The two characters are alike because they are both birds and they both live on the farm. They are different because the hen wants to work and the duck does not.

- **Summarize** Draw a large box with arrows going to several smaller boxes. Model how to select and write an important event or idea from the story in each smaller box. Then model how to use the information to write a brief summary in your own words. A summary for the passage shown might be: *A hen plants a grain of wheat by herself because the other animals will not help her.*

The Reading-Writing Connection

Writing about the words and pictures in a text is one of the best ways to clarify and apply the information and ideas. Students can extend and refine their comprehension through shared writing, interactive writing, or drawing and writing in a reading journal.

Here are some extension activities and question prompts based on a reading of *The Little Red Hen*.

Analyze a Character's Feelings Think about the hen. How did the hen feel when she found the grain of wheat? How did the hen feel when the other animals would not help her?

Analyze the Problem and Solution How did the hen solve her problem? How else could she solve the problem?

Analyze the Text What do you like best about the story? What do you dislike?

Describe a Character Think about your favorite character in the story. How would you describe the character to a friend?

Describe a Place Think about your favorite place in the story. How would you describe the place to a friend?

Make a Prediction Think about what the duck, dog, cat, and pig might do next time. Write about your prediction.

Persuade the Author Do you wish something different was in the story? Write a letter to the author about your idea. Then write why your idea would make the story better.

Piggyback Use some of the author's words, phrases, or sentence patterns to write your own story.

Retell Think about your favorite part of the story. Write about your favorite part in your own words.

Write a Description Imagine you are the hen. Write about the things you can see and hear. Write about how you feel, too.

Write a How-To Think about how to plant a seed. Write how to do it in your own words.

Write a Letter What would you like to say to the hen? What would you like to ask the hen? Share your thoughts by writing a letter to the hen.

Write a Personal Narrative Think about a time you asked someone for help. What happened?

Write a Summary Think about something you learned in the story. Write what you learned in your own words.

Reader Response Prompts

Students may respond to a text in many ways to demonstrate their comprehension.

- Act out something from the book with a partner.
- Draw a picture of _____. Then tell a partner why you drew it.
- Draw and label a picture of _____.
- Draw your favorite character. Use a speech bubble to show something the character might say.
- With a partner, draw several scenes from the story. Tape the scenes on the wall and use them to retell the story to the class.
- Name your favorite _____ in the book. Tell why you like it.
- Rate the book with a 1 (don't like), 2 (okay), or 3 (like a lot). Tell why you chose that rating.
- Tell something you learned in the book.
- Tell what you saw in your mind as you read.
- Tell what you wondered as you read.
- Tell something you already knew about _____.
- Tell about another book you have seen about _____.
- Tell how you think _____ learned _____.
- Tell how _____ might have felt when _____.
- Tell your favorite part of the book to a partner.
- Tell one way _____ and _____ are alike.
- Tell why you think the author included _____ in the book.
- Tell what you remember best about the book.
- Tell about your favorite page in the book.
- Tell about your favorite picture in the book.
- Use the pictures in the book to retell the story to a partner.
- Write a caption for one of the pictures.
- Write a word that describes each _____.
- Write a question you would like to ask _____.
- Write a question you would like to ask the author.
- Write about a connection you made to the book.
- Make a mural of the story.
- Write what you thought was most important in the book.

Fluency Mini-Lessons

Fluency is the ability to read a text accurately and quickly. When fluent readers read silently, they recognize words automatically. They group words quickly to help them gain meaning from what they read. Fluent readers read aloud effortlessly and with expression. Their reading sounds natural, as if they are speaking. Fluency provides a vital bridge between word recognition and comprehension. Because fluent readers do not have to concentrate on decoding words, they can focus attention on what the text means.

When modeling fluent reading for your students, consider these key areas:

Speed and Pacing Reading faster or slower to help show the meaning of the passage

Pausing Using the words and punctuation to figure out when to take a short or long break while reading

Inflection and Intonation Changing your voice (high or low, loud or soft) to help show the meaning of the passage; knowing when to emphasize certain words

Phrasing Reading related groups of words together to help the passage make sense

Expression Using different voices, facial expressions, and body language to help show the meaning of the passage

Accuracy Reading the words correctly

Integration Combining all the skills in a way that shows the reader understands the text

Students can practice reading fluently with the following activities based on the Big Book *Jack & the Beanstalk* by Brenda Parkes and Judith Smith. As always, use the gradual release of responsibility model by first thinking aloud and demonstrating the skill, then guiding students as they practice, and finally allowing them to try the activity with a partner or on their own while you are nearby to offer encouragement and support.

Rhythm Reading

Help students internalize the rhythm of a rhyming or repetitive text, such as Ogre's ranting on page 14. Once the children are familiar with the words, invite them to clap, snap their fingers, tap pencils, or use musical instruments as they read.

> The **Ogre** shouted,
> **Fee-fi-fo-fum,**
> I smell the blood
> of an Englishman.
> If he's alive, or if he's dead,
> I'll grind his bones
> to make my bread.

Text and Graphic Features

The following example shows one way a teacher helps students use the text feature bold print to guide their oral reading.

Teacher: I'm going to read pages 12 and 13 to you. Listen carefully. Then tell me what you think of my reading when I'm done. *(The teacher reads the pages in a flat voice.)*

Students: It sounded boring!

Teacher: Yes, it did! I can fix that, though. The author gives clues about how to read some of the words. The author uses bold print. Bold print is darker than regular print. What words are in bold print?

Russell: BANG BANG BANG.

Mary: Ogre.

Sy: GIGANTIC Ogre.

Teacher: You're exactly right! What else do you notice about some of the bold words?

David: Some of them have all uppercase letters.

Teacher: Yes, they do. I will read the bold words a little stronger and louder. I will read the bold words with all uppercase letters even stronger and louder. *(The teacher rereads the pages as described.)*

Students: That wasn't boring! That was scary!

Teacher: Yes! The author's clues helped me read the pages the right way. Now I will read one sentence at a time and you can try to say the words the same way. *(The students echo-read.)* Good work! Now let's read the pages together. *(The students choral-read with the teacher.)*

So the old woman took Jack into the kitchen. "Sit down," she said, "and I'll give you something to eat." But suddenly the floor began to shake!

BANG BANG BANG

"It's the **Ogre!**" said the old woman. "Quick! Get into the oven." Jack got into the oven just in time. The door flew open, and in strode a **GIGANTIC Ogre.**

Punctuation Marks

Periods Read the last three sentences on page 15 without pausing. Then read the sentences again, making a full stop at each period. Explain that stopping helps show that you have finished a complete thought.

> "There's no one here, except me," said the old woman.
> So the **Ogre** sat down at the table and the woman gave him some food.
> Jack lay **very very** still in the oven.
> He was **very very** frightened.

Read the sentences again, asking students to echo-read. Then choral-read the sentences with them, stopping at each period.

Commas Read the first sentence on page 3 without pausing. Then read the sentence again, pausing at the comma. Explain that pausing at the comma makes the sentence sound right.

> On the way to the market, Jack met an old woman.
> "Do you want to sell your cow?" she asked him.
> "Yes," said Jack.

Read the sentence again, asking students to echo-read. Then choral-read the sentence with them, pausing at the comma.

Question Marks On page 3, read the old woman's question in a flat voice, holding your hand level while you read it. Discuss how this makes the question sound.

> "Do you want to sell your cow?" she asked him.

Then read the question again, moving your hand upward at the end as you move your voice to a higher pitch. Ask students to echo-read and move their hands along with yours. Choral-read the question with them, moving to a higher pitch at the end.

Exclamation Points Read the first two sentences on page 13 in a flat voice. Discuss how this makes the listener feel. Then read the sentences again, saying the exclamations more quickly and in a higher pitch.

> "It's the **Ogre!**" said the old woman.
> "Quick! Get into the oven."
> Jack got into the oven just in time.
> The door flew open, and in strode a **GIGANTIC Ogre**.

Ask students to echo-read. Choral-read the sentences with them, using a faster, higher voice for the exclamations.

Bibliography

Beck, I. L., L. Kucan, and M. G. McKeown. *Bringing Words to Life: Robust Vocabulary Instruction.* New York: Guilford Press, 2002.

Calkins, L. *The Art of Teaching Reading.* New York: Longman, 2001: 266–267, 300.

Dorn, L. J., C. French, and T. Jones. *Apprenticeship in Literacy: Transitions Across Reading and Writing.* Portland, ME: Stenhouse, 1998.

Fisher, B., and E. Medvic. *Perspectives on Shared Reading: Planning and Practice.* Portsmouth, NH: Heinemann, 2000.

Holdaway, D. *The Foundations of Literacy.* Sydney, Australia: Ashton Scholastic, 1979.

Marzano, R. J., and D. J. Pickering. *Building Academic Vocabulary: Teacher's Manual.* Alexandria, VA: Association for Supervision and Curriculum Development, 2005.

Mooney, M. E. *Reading To, With, and By Children.* Katonah, NY: Richard C. Owen Publishers, 1990: 25–39.

Osborn, J., and F. Lehr. *Literacy for All: Issues in Teaching and Learning.* New York: Guilford Press, 1998.

Parkes, B. *Read It Again!: Revisiting Shared Reading.* Portland, ME: Stenhouse, 2000.

Routman, R. *Invitations: Changing as Teachers and Learners, K-12.* Portsmouth, NH: Heinemann, 1994: 33–38.

Vacca, J., et al. *Reading and Learning to Read.* 2nd ed. New York: Harper Collins, 1991: 80–83.